Giant Pandas

AnnMarie
Anderson

SCHOLASTIC INC.

Bao Bao is a giant panda. She lives at the National Zoo in Washington, D.C.

Bao Bao
[bough BOUGH]
means
"precious treasure"
in Chinese.

Giant pandas are
special animals.
They are **endangered**.

*There are fewer
than 2,500 giant
pandas living
today.*

Giant pandas are **mammals**.
Mammals are **warm-blooded**
animals. They have fur or hair.
Mammal mothers make
milk for their babies
to drink.

These are
other kinds
of mammals.

elephant

whale

dog

human

NEW WORD

mammal

MAM-uhl

A **mammal** is a warm-blooded animal that gives birth to live babies.

SAY IT OUT LOUD

7

Giant pandas are related to bears. They have many things in common. Bears have sharp teeth and claws. So do Pandas.

panda teeth

panda claws

They both like
to climb trees.

But bears and pandas are also different. Most bears **hibernate**. Giant pandas do not. Pandas also do not hunt or roar.

black bear

polar bear

brown bear

If giant pandas want
to say hello, they bleat.

They sound like
sheep or baby goats.

Most bears eat meat.
But giant pandas eat
a plant called **bamboo**.

A special
bump
on the bear's
paw works
like a thumb. ......

It makes it easy
for a giant panda
to grab and
eat bamboo.

A giant panda spends half the day eating. Some eat 40 pounds of bamboo in one day.

To eat 40 pounds of ice cream, you would have to eat about 35 pints!

In the wild, giant pandas
live in bamboo forests.
These forests are
in the mountains
of central China.

China

Bamboo
Forests

But not all giant pandas live in China. Some live in zoos in other countries.

RUTH HARKNESS

In 1936, an American **explorer** named Ruth brought the first giant panda to the United States. Su Lin was the first panda to leave China. He lived at the Brookfield Zoo in Chicago, Illinois.

No matter where they live, giant pandas eat bamboo. But in zoos, giant pandas get other food, too.

Some of these foods include carrots, apples, sweet potatoes, and ice pops made with frozen fruit!

carrots

Xiao Liwu
[sh-yow-lee-woo]
("little gift" in Chinese)
lives at the
San Diego Zoo.

apples

sweet potatoes

ice pops

Giant panda babies are born in the late summer or early fall.

A mother has one or two **cubs** at a time. When they are born, the cubs are tiny and pink. They do not have fur yet.

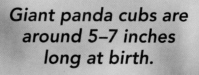

Giant panda cubs are around 5–7 inches long at birth.

4 5 6 7

Cubs do not open their eyes until they are about six weeks old.

Giant panda cubs start to walk when they are about three months old.

They stay with their mothers until they are at least a year and a half old.

Scientists study giant pandas.

They know that pandas like to spend time in small groups.

Would you like to see
a giant panda?
You are in luck!

Many zoos have
"panda cams."

You can get a peek
at these animals
right from your computer.

Smile and say
cheese, Bao Bao!

Glossary

bamboo
A tropical plant with a hollow, woody stem.

cub
A young animal, such as a lion, wolf, or bear.

endangered
Someone or something in a dangerous situation.

explorer
A person who travels and looks around to discover things.

hibernate
To sleep for the entire winter. Some animals, like bears, do this.

mammal
A warm-blooded animal that has hair or fur and usually gives birth to live babies. Female mammals produce milk to feed their young.

scientist
A person who is trained and works in science.

warm-blooded
When an animal has a warm body temperature that does not change according to the temperature around it.

Index

ISBN 978-0-545-93549-4

10 9 8 7 6 5 4 3 2   16 17 18 19 20

Printed in the U.S.A. 40
First printing, July 2016

5